IMAGES
of America

UPPER ST. CLAIR

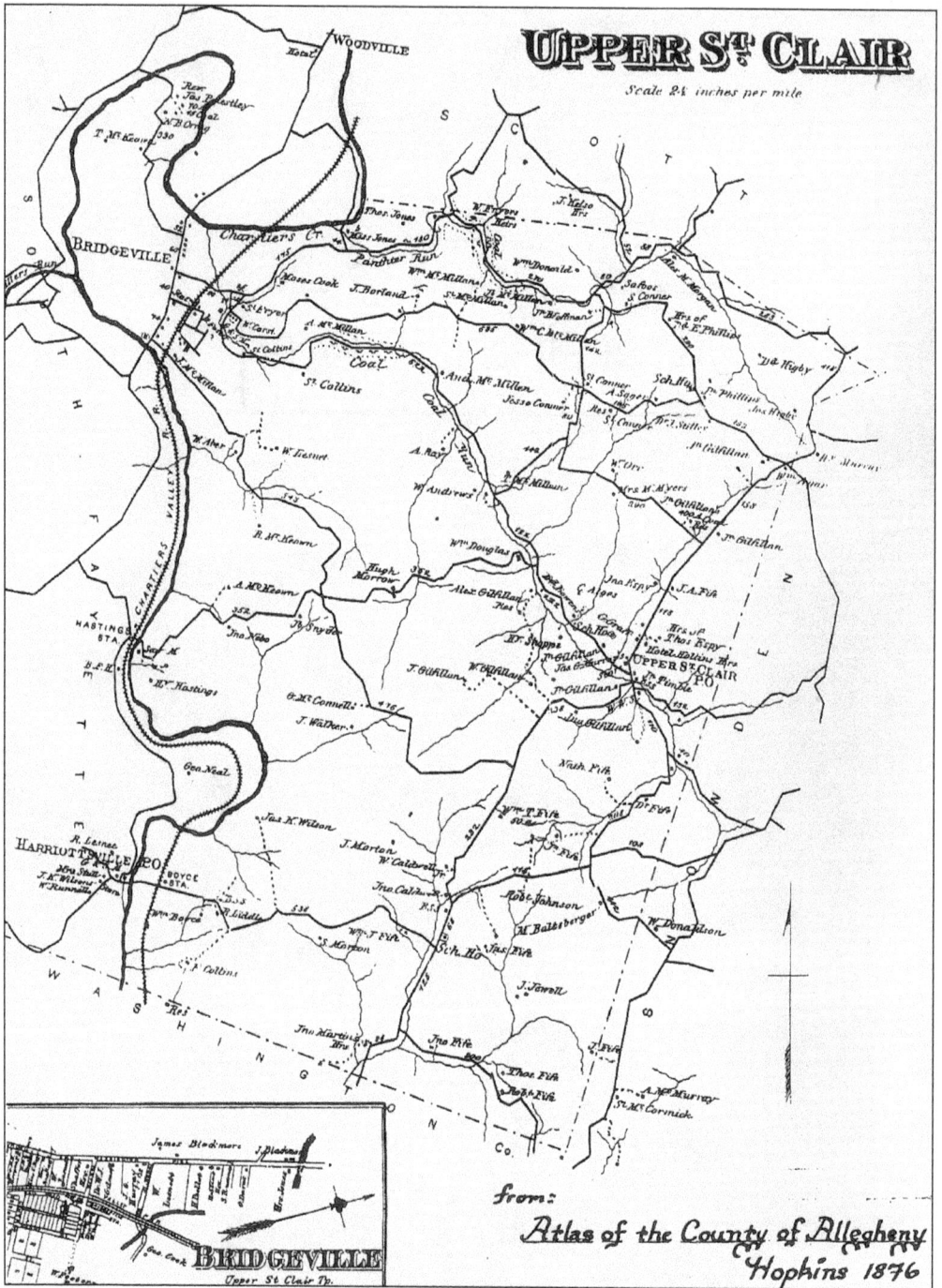

The holdings of landowners in Upper St. Clair Township are shown on this 1876 map, which is found in *Atlas of the County of Allegheny*.

IMAGES
of *America*

UPPER ST. CLAIR

Upper St. Clair Historical Society
Larry R. Godwin

ARCADIA
PUBLISHING

Published by Arcadia Publishing
Charleston, South Carolina

Library of Congress Catalog Card Number: 2001090999

For all general information contact Arcadia Publishing at:
Telephone 843-853-2070
Fax 843-853-0044
E-mail sales@arcadiapublishing.com
For customer service and orders:
Toll-Free 1-888-313-2665

Visit us on the Internet at www.arcadiapublishing.com

Upper St. Clair Township was named for Arthur St. Clair (1736–1818). A native of Thurso, Scotland, St. Clair was a major general in the Revolutionary War. He served as president of the Continental Congress in 1787 and was the first governor of the Northwest Territory, which was located between the Ohio and Mississippi Rivers.

CONTENTS

ACKNOWLEDGMENTS

We would like to thank all of the people who contributed to the preparation and production of this work. We are grateful to all who shared treasured photographs and memories to help in this endeavor, especially the members of the Bridgeville Centennial Committee for their important contributions. A very special thanks is extended to Jean G. Brown and to Dorothy P. Holden of the Upper St. Clair Historical Society, who labored on this project from beginning to end, without whose help this book could not have been produced. And finally, we gratefully acknowledge the historical accounts written by the late Margaret Gilfillan, to whom this book is dedicated.

INTRODUCTION

Upper St. Clair Township was named in honor of Arthur St. Clair, a major general during the American Revolution. He came to America from Scotland as a British ensign to fight in the French and Indian War. After purchasing 4,000 acres in Westmoreland County, St. Clair was appointed by Governor Penn to numerous local political offices. He supported Pennsylvania's claim to the territory west of the Monongahela River against Virginia's claim to the same land. Following the Revolution, St. Clair served as president of the Continental Congress and later served as governor of the Northwest Territory. St. Clair was relieved of his duties by Pres. Thomas Jefferson after suffering a defeat in a battle with Native Americans.

The area was originally located in Yohogania County, District of West Augusta, Virginia. At the same time, the Penn family claimed the land for Pennsylvania. When Virginia gave up its claim to the Northwest Territory in 1784, this land became part of Peters Township, Washington County, Pennsylvania. In 1788, Allegheny County was carved from parts of Washington and Westmoreland Counties and was divided into seven townships, one of which was named St. Clair. Its boundaries were the Monongahela River in the north, Washington County in the south, Streets Run in the east, and Chartiers Creek in the west. St. Clair Township was divided into Lower and Upper St. Clair in 1806. The term "upper" referred to the higher elevation as one traveled south, away from the Monongahela River. Upper St. Clair Township was subsequently divided into the present townships of Scott, Mount Lebanon, and South Park. It was divided into the boroughs of Baldwin, Bethel Park, Bridgeville, Castle Shannon, Crafton, Dormont, Greentree, Ingram, and part of Carnegie. It also included nine wards of the city of Pittsburgh.

Early settlers received patents for their land from either Pennsylvania or Virginia, depending on which state he thought had legal right to the territory. The first known settler here was John Fife of Fifeshire, Scotland, who was believed to have arrived in 1762. His first Pennsylvania land patent was called Cremona, and he later acquired two smaller tracts, which were named Lambeth and Fife's Utility. Other early settlers and their land patents were Richard Boyce, Content; Cornelius Connor, Difficulty; Alexander Fowler, Wingfield; Alexander Gilfillan, Cato; James Morrow, Mill Grove; John Neville, Sidgefield; Adam Patterson, Trouble Without Profit; and Joseph Philips, Ugly. Most of these settlers came from England, Scotland, and Northern Ireland, the latter being known as Scotch-Irish.

For most of Upper St. Clair's existence, farming has been the main occupation of its citizens. Farmers here received national attention in 1794 when they conducted an insurrection against a federal tax on whiskey makers. It was more profitable for farmers to turn their corn and rye crops into whiskey, which could be more easily shipped to market, than to transport bulky grain. The federal law permitted government agents to enter homes and collect money from small whiskey producers. Nearly 500 angry farmers gathered at Fort Couch on July 15, 1794, and marched along the ridge of Fort Couch Road to Gen. John Neville's home at Bower Hill with the intention of burning it down. Pres. George Washington sent in troops to stop the rebellion. Two rebel leaders were convicted of treason but were later pardoned by Washington. The Whiskey Rebellion was an early test of the use of federal power within a state to enforce a federal law.

Upper St. Clair had an organized militia during most of the period between the Revolution and the Civil War. When Pres. Abraham Lincoln called for volunteers, Thomas Espy of Clifton organized and became captain of the St. Clair Guards. On July 25, 1861, 83 men were mustered into service as Company H, 62nd Regiment of the Pennsylvania Volunteers. They served with honor and distinction through the Civil War. Thirteen members of the St. Clair Guards were killed, including Captain Espy, who died at Gaines Mill.

As the township flourished in the 1800s, villages sprang up along the streams. They were Clifton, earlier known as "Sodom," along McLaughlin Run; Beadling, located along Painters Run; and Boyce Station and Bridgeville, both of which are located along Chartiers Creek. Bridgeville became the largest of these villages. Two railroads served Bridgeville, and Washington Pike—the main route between Pittsburgh and Washington—passed through. It had the greatest concentration of people and was the economic and social center of Upper St. Clair until it became a borough in 1901. Bridgeville continued to annex areas from Upper St. Clair until 1951, when it acquired residential neighborhoods along the north side of Lesnett Road, Bower Hill Road, and Bridgemont, as well as Cook School, which it purchased from the township. Coal mining became important in the development of Beadling. Several hundred miners and their families lived and worked in Beadling from 1883 to when the mines closed in 1923. Clifton is, at the present time, considered to be the hub of Upper St. Clair.

Early schools were named for the landowner who offered property for the construction of a one-room school. The Higbee School, on the Higbee farm in the northeast corner of Upper St. Clair, was the first public school west of the Allegheny Mountains. Other one-room schools on farmers' land were Caldwell School, Lesnett School, Philips School, and St. Clair School, which was always known as the "school in the woods" and was located on the Espy farm. In the late 1800s, the one-room schools were replaced by two-room schools named Bridgeville, Cook, Clifton, and McMillen. New and larger schools were constructed in the 1920s. They, too, were named Cook, Clifton, and McMillen. It was at this time that students began riding to school by bus. In 1951, Fort Couch School was built to accommodate all Upper St. Clair students from kindergarten through grade eight. Throughout the 1950s, students continued to attend high school at Bridgeville or Mount Lebanon. Late in that decade, high school classes were added. The only classes to graduate from high school at Fort Couch School were in 1960, 1961, and 1962. The Upper St. Clair High School was opened in September 1962, and the first class graduated from the new building in 1963. From humble beginnings, Upper St. Clair schools have earned a national reputation for excellence in education.

The transformation to the suburban community that we know today began in 1913 with the opening of the Brookside Farms development on the Alfred Fife farm. It was located along the Pittsburgh-to-Washington interurban trolley line and near the St. Clair Country Club. The developer, Freehold Real Estate Company, promised "interurban refinement and social eminence." That statement set the standard for future development in Upper St. Clair. With the opening of the Liberty Tubes in the 1920s, the South Hills land rush began. Trotwood Acres, Southern Hilands, English Village, Ruthfred Acres, and St. Clair Acres soon followed. With continued residential development and a population of approximately 20,000, Upper St. Clair is recognized as a premier community in which to live. We love Upper St. Clair today, and we love to remember the way it was.

One

FRIENDS AND FAMILIES

This is a composite picture of Upper St. Clair residents. Do you know who they are?

William T. Fife built the large brick home on Old Washington Road in 1840.

John T. Fife and his daughter Lulu enjoy sitting in their garden.

James and Margaret Morgan Fife were married on December 1, 1870. Their home on Fife Drive was built as a wedding present.

Wilson Lesnett, who was born in 1808, was the grandson of Christian Lesnett of Germany, the first member of the family to live in this area.

Thomas Dell and Martha Lesnett visit the Schneiders at their new home on Morrow Road in 1941.

Thomas Dell Lesnett and Martha Virginia enjoy apples together.

Belle (left) and Abbie, daughters of William and Clarinda Lesnett, sit on their porch for a photograph in 1900. Later, Belle married Harry Schneider, and Abbie married James Morrow.

The Schneider family gathers for a family photograph in 1945. From left to right are the following: (front row) Belle, Harry, and Clarinda Smith holding son Harry; (back row) Jim, Dick, Bill, Ed, and Bill Smith.

Frank Williams (left) and his father, John, are shown in their orchard in the 1890s.

Seen in this late-1890s portrait of Frank Williams's children are, from left to right, Charlie, Clifford, and Wesley.

Isaac and Jane Cox of Hickman Street in Bridgeville pose for a portrait.

Jane Cox (seated) and her children gather on the porch of their Hickman Street home. From left to right are Isaac, Samuel, Benjamin, Roseanna, and James.

The Orient family lines up in 1937 for a family picture at their home on McLaughlin Run Road. They are, from left to right, Joe, Bill, Catherine (mother), John, Beatrice, Paul, Jim, George, and Florine.

The Barkand family of Morrow Road poses for a family portrait. They are, from left to right, as follows: (front row, sitting) Peg, Emma (mother), and Hilda; (back row, standing) Emily, Bill, Otto, Emma, Carl, Earl, and Mildred.

Mrs. J. Peter Hoffman summoned everyone to dinner by blowing the horn. This photograph was taken at her home on Fort Couch Road c. 1900.

The J. Peter Hoffman family is shown on the porch of their family home on Fort Couch Road.

John H. and Louise Hoffman lived on McMillan Road behind St. John Capistran Church. Their farm is now the Fox Chase development. Their daughter Clara was postmistress of the Beadling post office. John Hoffman constructed the small building that housed the post office. Another daughter, Agnes, was an active member of the Upper St. Clair Historical Society.

Bub Scott (left) operated a blacksmith shop on North Highland Road across from the Williams home. He is pictured with one of the McEwen brothers.

Margaret McEwen (seated) of Locust Lane and her sons pose for a portrait. From left to right are Roy, John, Frank, Will, Kiefer, Allen, and George.

These portraits of Alexander and Margaret (Aiken) Gilfillan were taken in the late 1850s. They lived in the home on Swanson Lane.

Twins Nellie and Helen Currie are shown on an outing in 1913 with younger brothers Andy, Bob, and Clark.

Alexander Gilfillan and his children are shown c. 1913. The children are, from left to right, Alexander, Margaret, and John.

Charles and Sarah Godwin founded C. Godwin & Sons in 1898. They are pictured here in one of their greenhouses, surrounded by flower beds.

Arthur Godwin introduces Elmer the bull to his grandson Terry Williard. This pasture is where the Rolling Meadows development is now located.

Dominic Palombo Sr. was the founder of South Hills Nurseries, on North Highland Road.

Mrs. Dominic Palombo supervises children playing in the yard.

Two

HOMES

The Webb Murray house, on Washington Avenue in Bridgeville, was built in 1898. Pictured, from left to right, are Mrs. W.W. Murray, Mrs. A.B. Murray, Alberta, Jim, Sam, and an unidentified bicyclist.

"Jonathan's Folly" was constructed in 1830 by Jonathan Middlesworth for his 16-year-old bride-to-be, Mary McKown. After being jilted by his fiancée, Middlesworth lived in virtual seclusion, with his mother, in the mansion. Pictured here are A.B. Murray and family, who purchased the home in 1901. For many years, this house was the social hub of Bridgeville. It was razed in 1956, and the site is now a parking lot next to PNC Bank.

The George P. Murray home, on Washington Avenue in Bridgeville, was erected in 1896. It was located on the current site of the Bridgeville post office parking lot.

The Samuel Foster home, on Station Street in Bridgeville, was built in 1898. From the front porch, activities at the Norwood Hotel, located across the street, could be observed.

The Donaldson home—in Greenwood Place, Bridgeville—was built in 1799.

This 1900 photograph shows the home of Charles and Sarah Godwin, on Mayview Road. Greenhouses are seen in the background.

Reflected in the pond is the home of George and Ida May Poellot, on Boyce Road.

The W.W. Lesnett home still stands on Lesnett Road. Pictured, from left to right, are William W. Lesnett; his daughter Belle; and his wife, Clarinda. The landmark octagonal barn is seen in the background.

The Baldesberger home, on McMurray Road, was purchased by St. Louise de Marillac Church in 1961.

The Borland house, on Cook School Road, was built in the 1850s. The house belongs to members of the Bedner family, who continue to operate the farm.

The William Caldwell house, on McLaughlin Run Road, was occupied by Clarence and Mary Caldwell and Edna Fife and her sons.

The John L. Poellot farm, on McMurray Road at Clifton, is now the site of Outback Steakhouse. On the hill in the distance is "the school in the woods."

The stagecoach inn at Clifton was owned by the John Gilfillan family. It was later occupied by the family of Jack Klancher, Upper St. Clair's first police chief.

The McMillen home, on McMillan Road, was last occupied by the family of Lee and Ann Beck.

The Ellsworth Phillips home was located on Washington Road near the Clifton cloverleaf. The home was built in the early 1900s.

A steam locomotive passes near Brookside Farms. The Nathan Couch farm on Kennebec Road is seen on the hill.

The landmark home of Harry and Lydia Boyce still stands next to the railroad at Boyce Station. Harry Boyce is standing in front of the fence in this photograph.

The Fred Boyce home stood on the site of Frosty Valley Golf Club on Boyce Road.

The two homes on this page are Sears, Roebuck catalog mail-order homes. Sears produced more than 100,000 homes between 1908 and 1940. The company shipped precut lumber and materials by rail throughout the United States. The Currie home (above), on Johnston Road, was constructed in 1929 in the bungalow style. The English cottage–style home of the Smith family (above), on Morrow Road, was built in 1939.

The James Espy farm was located on Washington Road near Clifton.

The Strickler DeMuth home, c. 1881, stands at the corner of Hays Road and Lindenwood Drive.

The John Gilfillan house on Washington Road, *c.* 1857, is constructed of bricks made on the site. It is now owned by the Upper St. Clair Historical Society.

Alexander and Margaret Gilfillan's home, located on Swanson Lane, was built in 1865.

The Henry May home and dairy farm was located in the Somerville Drive area.

The Pittsburgh Coal Company erected houses for the miners and their families at Beadling.

The Alexander Gilfillan cabin, built in 1783, stood at the site of the present St. Clair Country Club clubhouse.

The Orient log house, on Morrow Road, was located near the township tennis courts.

The J. Peter Hoffman home, built in 1880, is located on Fort Couch Road.

The home of John H. and Louise Hoffman was located behind McMillen School and, later, St. John Capistran Church. Agnes Hoffman was the last occupant.

This c. 1900 photograph shows the home of Joseph and Katherina Orient on Cook School Road. The most recent owners of the house were Louis and Nelle Delach.

The Michael Orient home was located on Cook School Road. The last occupants were Martha and Lucy Orient.

The Sam Fife house, on Old Washington Road, was constructed in 1878 and was razed in 1959. It was located at the current site of the Christian and Missionary Alliance Church.

The William T. Fife house, on Old Washington Road, has long been a landmark. It was built in 1840.

The Albert T. Fife home, located at the corner of Old Washington and Hastings Mill Roads, was constructed in 1908.

James Fife and his daughter Margaret stand in front of their home on Fife Drive. The house was constructed in 1870.

The Johnston home, on Southvue Drive, was built in 1838 with bricks made on site.

The 1820 home of Thomas Dell and Martha Lesnett is located on Old Lesnett Road. The house is still occupied by members of the Lesnett family.

This is the 1830 log house as it looked in 1913 (above) and as it looks now after being restored to its original appearance (below).

The Joseph Philips house on Seeger Road, *c.* 1806, is the oldest home in Upper St. Clair.

The Orr home, on Murdstone Road, was erected in 1857.

The John McEwen home, on Locust Lane, was constructed in 1892.

John Williams (born in 1828) drives past his home on North Highland Road.

The 1847 Quigg house still stands on Fort Couch Road at the corner of Quigg Drive.

The R.R. King farm, known as Elmbrook, was located near Johnston Road.

The Stockdale home, on Orr Road, is pictured c. 1940. Being at the crest of the hill and surrounded by meadows, it is a landmark that can be seen from numerous locations in Upper St. Clair.

Three

SCHOOLS

The Higbee School, in the northeast corner of the township, was constructed in 1794 and was the first public school west of the Allegheny Mountains. It was restored and moved to Mount Lebanon Park in the 1930s. It was razed in the 1960s.

The Class of 1886–1887 gathers in front of Bridgeville Public School on Hickman Street. Josie Couch (labeled here as No. 3) was the teacher. The school is now a private residence.

This photograph of students at the Lesnett School was taken *c.* 1900. The school was located where Montclair is today.

The Philips School (above) was built in 1888 on Fort Couch Road where the school bus garage is located today. The Hoffman cousins (below) are shown standing at the school's entrance. They are, from left to right, Mary, Clara, Margaret, Lucy, and Regina.

The boys at the Caldwell School on Old Washington Road are seen here with their teacher, Ben Cronessner. The school is now a private residence.

This class picture was taken at the first Clifton School *c.* 1908.

The first Clifton School, which contained two rooms, was built in 1890. It was replaced by the new Clifton School in 1920, which was constructed of brick.

Ora Bell (left) and Charlotte Wright pose with their students at the first Clifton School.

Teachers stand in front of the old McMillen School, which was constructed in 1894. It is shown here following an addition that increased its size to four classrooms. The school was destroyed by fire in 1924 and was replaced by a new brick school.

The new McMillen School, erected in 1924, replaced the old frame building. It is now occupied by St. John Capistran Church.

Students assemble in front of the first Cook School on Bower Hill Road *c.* 1910. Today, the building is a private residence.

The entire student body of Cook School poses in this 1940s portrait. Alfred F. Baker, superintendent, stands to the left of the Upper St. Clair Honor Roll. Cook School was purchased by the Borough of Bridgeville in 1951.

Seen here are Clifton School teachers on an outing. They are, from left to right, as follows: (front row, sitting) Charlotte Wright and Catherine Ballentine Nordseick; (back row, standing) Sadie Himmeger and Sara Lesnett.

Sara Lesnett's Class of 1929–1930 poses in front of Clifton School.

The Clifton School student body is arranged in front of the school in this 1930s portrait. The teachers on the lower porch are, from left to right, Sadie Himmeger, Charlotte Wright, Catherine Ballentine Nordseick, and Sara Lesnett.

Students began riding school buses to Clifton, McMillen, and Cook schools in the early 1920s. Drivers were Shorty Reid and Skip Walther. Note that the school bus was black.

Emma Hoffman and her 1927–1928 class pose in front of McMillen School.

This 1949 photograph of George Betcher (left) in his first year as physical education teacher and Alfred F. Baker, supervising principal, was taken on the athletic field at Clifton School.

First- and second-graders at McMillen School pose in this 1941 photograph with their teacher, Emma Hoffman.

This is the new Fort Couch School, completed in 1951, which replaced Clifton, McMillen, and Cook Schools. It cost $650,000 and accommodated 650 students from kindergarten through grade eight. There was no high school at this time, so Upper St. Clair students attended either Mount Lebanon High School or Bridgeville High School. Upper St. Clair's first three classes of high school seniors graduated from Fort Couch School in 1960, 1961, and 1962.

Upper St. Clair's first public kindergarten opened in 1951 in the new Fort Couch School. Helen W. Fulton was the teacher.

Margaret Pearson's second-grade class poses for a group picture at the new Fort Couch School during the 1951–1952 school year.

Bruce Kiefer, music director at Fort Couch School, poses with the 1952–1953 band (above) and chorus (below).

Dolores Merritt coached the girls' junior high basketball team in 1952–1953.

The 1952–1953 boys' junior high basketball team was coached by George Betcher.

Tola Poellot was the librarian at the Upper St. Clair schools for many years. She served at Cook, McMillen, Clifton, Fort Couch, and Upper St. Clair High Schools. She is seated in the center of the front row in this picture of the Fort Couch Library Aides.

Industrial arts students at Fort Couch School pose with their teacher, Charles Templeton.

Students respond to questions in Joseph Argiro's biology class. Active in student affairs, Argiro coached the first high school baseball team.

Paul Pavlov instructs high school art students in this early-1960s photograph. Artwork produced here brightened the hallways and display cases of the high school.

Upper St. Clair High School was opened in September 1962. It was constructed at a cost of $2,765,000 on 25 acres of land purchased from the Gilfillans. The Class of 1963 was the first class to graduate from this school.

Lisa Holden (front, center) was a second-grader in 1969 when she performed as the mascot for the Upper St. Clair High School Pantherettes.

Angelo Ruzzini (left) was the director of the Upper St. Clair High School Band. They are assembled in the band room of the new high school in this 1963 photograph.

Upper St. Clair school district administrators are pictured here in the late 1960s. From left to right are Mr. George Betcher, Dr. Niles Norman, and Dr. Donald Eichhorn.

The 1963–1964 Upper St. Clair High School senior class is assembled for a group portrait with class sponsor John Wasson (third row, far right).

Four

FARMS, MINES, AND BUSINESSES

This 1970s photograph shows Alexander Gilfillan feeding his sheep at the family farm on Washington Road.

The W.W. Lesnett family is seen in front of their landmark octagonal barn, on Lesnett Road. They are, from left to right, Belle, Clarinda, and William W.

The 1868 Gilfillan barn, on Washington Road, is still in use housing sheep and goats.

Farm workers build a haystack on the Espy farm, on Washington Road.

Family members and hired workers bale hay on the Sam Fife farm, on Old Washington Road.

The Godwin smokestack has been a landmark since it was erected in 1929. C. Godwin & Sons was founded on Mayview Road in 1898 and is the oldest business in Upper St. Clair.

This 1904 photograph shows the Godwin family, their home, and their greenhouses. From left to right are Miriam (on the porch), Arthur (in the wagon), Frank, Charles Jr. and wife Elizabeth, and Charles Sr. and wife Sarah.

This 1950 aerial view of C. Godwin & Sons shows the development of the Lesnett-Mayview Road area. The new homes that are in the upper left corner of this photograph, on the north side of Lesnett Road, were soon to be annexed by the Borough of Bridgeville. Lesnett Road became the dividing line between Upper St. Clair and Bridgeville in 1951.

South Hills Nurseries, founded by Dominic Palombo, was located between Washington and North Highland Roads. Andrew Palombo stands by a fleet of trucks in this early-1940s photograph. Today, the business is in the same location and continues to be managed by the Palombo family.

The Schaffer Woolen Mill was in operation on Washington Avenue in Bridgeville in the 1850s and 1860s. During the Civil War, men gathered in the factory office to discuss politics and war news.

Oxen were used to do heavy work at the sawmill along McLaughlin Run at Clifton in the late 1800s.

The Brookside Farms development was named for this picturesque brook near the streetcar stop. Residential building began in 1913 and continued until the 1980s.

This early-1920s view of Brookside Farms shows homes on Comanche, Apache, Arapahoe, and Sioux Roads.

This 1940 scene along Old Washington Road shows the windmill building that served as a real estate office for the Southern Hilands development.

In this 1962 view of the entrance to Westminster Manor, the first home belonging to Donald and Jean Brown can be seen.

This view of Mayview State Hospital was taken from Morton Road. It was founded in the mid-1800s and was originally called Marshalsea.

Everyone is on hand at the J.B. McNay Grocery Store as the steam locomotive pulls into Boyce Station.

The E.E. Phillips Grocery Store, post office, warehouse, and Odd Fellows Lodge are seen in this turn-of-the-century scene at Clifton. Mr. and Mrs. Ellsworth Phillips are in the wagon.

Seen here is McCool's Service Station at Clifton in the 1930s. The establishment was famous for pies and penny candy. Notice that Washington Road had only two lanes and that McLaughlin Run and McMurray Roads were not connected.

The Hamel Mortuary, on McMurray Road, was established in 1947. All of Upper St. Clair's emergency calls came in on the "red phone" and were answered by Mr. and Mrs. Milton Hamel.

The J.L. Poellot Hardware and Wagon Shop at Clifton was a popular local gathering place. Pictured here are Dr. Fife (in the dark suit) and John Lewis Poellot (holding the horse). The Poellot children are, from left to right, Sarah (in the doorway), Annie (in the window), John Lewis II, Mary, Harry, unidentified, and Cleophus.

G. W. POELLOT.   ESTABLISHED 1888   W. H. POELLOT.

H. POELLOT'S SONS,
DEALERS IN

STOVES, RANGES,
GRANITE WARE,
MECHANICS'
AND FARMERS'
TOOLS.

HARDWARE

TINWARE,
BUILDERS' SUPPLIES,
HOUSE FURNISHING
GOODS,
GAS LAMPS,
BURNERS & MANTLES.

PAINTS, OILS,
VARNISHES.

Bridgeville, Pa.

Bell Phone, 36 J.

H. Poellot's Sons Hardware was established on Washington Avenue in Bridgeville in 1888. Pictured below are the proprietors, William Poellot (left) and George Washington Poellot. They were known to family and friends as "Will and Wash."

86

Two views of the intersection of Station and Railroad Streets in Bridgeville show the train station, S.A. Foster's store, and the Norwood Hotel. The above winter scene was taken in 1887. The photograph below shows the parklike grounds surrounding the Norwood Hotel.

The W.J. Winstein Store was on the corner of Washington Avenue and Bower Hill Road in Bridgeville. This photograph shows a group gathered at the store in 1888.

This 1899 Bridgeville photograph shows the shops in the center of town at Washington Avenue and Station Street. These buildings were destroyed by fire in 1960.

The Bennett Drug Store, on Washington Avenue in Bridgeville, served as the post office for Upper St. Clair. Pictured, from left to right, are Lydia Hodgekiss, William Bennett, and John Bennett.

This view of Essen shows the company store and miners' residences. Essen was located in the Painters Run valley downstream from Beadling.

In the above photograph, Clara Hoffman, postmistress at the Beadling post office, shows a poster to Karen and Linda Luxbacher. Below, Hoffman watches a worker measure the small post office building. These photographs were taken in the 1950s.

Here are two scenes of Beadling showing the coal-mining industry there. Above, miners pose with the mules that pulled coal cars through the mines. Below, railroad cars are being loaded with coal, and men congregate on Painters Run Road.

These two *c.* 1900 scenes show Beadling during the coal-mining era.

This view, looking toward Mount Lebanon, shows Robb Hollow Road. The Upper St. Clair Hotel is on the left.

Patrons, employees, and members of the Beadling baseball team pose in front of the Upper St. Clair Hotel, at the corner of Painters Run and Robb Hollow Roads. The hotel was later known as Walt's Tavern and is now called Painters Run.

Five

CHURCHES AND
ORGANIZATIONS

The 1953–1954 Beadling soccer team celebrates after winning the National Amateur Soccer Cup.

Police Chief Jack Klancher (right) and Dave Reebel met at Bud & Win's Lunches on Washington Road near Mitchell's Corner.

Members of the Upper St. Clair Police Department in the 1960s are, from left to right, Harold Buttlar, Donald Daugherty, Chief Jack Klancher, William Schubert, and William Buttlar.

Police Chief Jack Klancher walks on unpaved Fort Couch Road in the 1930s. Mitchell's Corner is seen in the distance.

Chief Jack Klancher directs traffic while standing next to his 1956 Dodge police cruiser.

Members of the Upper St. Clair Volunteer Fire Department pose in front of their fire truck in 1939. The truck was kept in a garage at Mitchell's Corner.

The Upper St. Clair Firemen's Ladies Auxiliary marched in a parade at the South Park Fairgrounds during the 1954 Allegheny County Fair.

The Upper St. Clair Township Volunteer Fire Department benefited from the 1940 horse show at Elmbrook on the R.R. King property.

This was the Upper St. Clair Volunteer Fire Department fire truck in the 1930s.

Web Connor delivered mail to Upper St. Clair from the Bridgeville post office. Connor and his mail wagon are seen in front of "Jonathan's Folly" on Washington Avenue in Bridgeville.

The Clifton Ladies Social Circle visited the H.J. Heinz complex on Pittsburgh's North Side in October 1912. It was the home of Heinz 57 Varieties.

Bethel Presbyterian Church was founded by the Reverend John McMillan in 1776. This 1856 building preceded the present church, which was built in 1910. Dr. Cornelius Wycoff, pictured here, was the pastor from 1873 to 1913.

The Beadling Presbyterian Chapel, on Cedar Boulevard, was a mission of Bethel Presbyterian Church. It was built in 1892 on land donated by the Gilkeson family.

St. Agatha Parish was formed in 1894. Services were held in a storeroom on Washington Avenue in Bridgeville until this church was constructed in 1900.

The St. John Capistran Church, on McMillan Road, was a mission of St. Agatha Parish in Bridgeville. This building was dedicated on December 23, 1923.

Bethany Presbyterian Church of Bridgeville was formed in 1886 with the union of two congregations. The church building shown here was constructed in 1889 on Washington Avenue near the south bridge over Chartiers Creek. It was on the same site as the large frame church, which had been called the "Lord's Barn."

This is an interior view of the 1889 Bethany Presbyterian Church.

The Bethany Presbyterian Church manse was erected in 1877 next door to the "Lord's Barn."

Westminster Presbyterian Church was organized after World War II. John H. Galbreath, a recently discharged Marine Corps chaplain, was the first pastor. He served in that capacity for 33 years. The first service was held at Clifton School (above) in September 1946. Ground was broken for the new church building (below) in August 1948.

Six

LEISURE

The Norwood Hotel in Bridgeville, constructed in 1876, was a luxury resort for prominent Pittsburgh businessmen and their families. Because the hotel was located near the railroad station, businessmen could easily commute to downtown offices and spend evenings among the beautiful gardens and shady pathways at the resort. Joseph Wright, the proprietor, encouraged guests to enjoy the healthful water from nearby Brandy's spring.

St. Clair Country Club was chartered in 1916. The first clubhouse was a farmhouse. It was replaced in 1919 by a new frame clubhouse (above), which was destroyed by fire in 1929. The present clubhouse (pictured below in 1939) was built by Ab Young, a general contractor, at a cost of $95,635.

Lawrence Hofrichter (left) and Thomas Bewick were members of the Beadling Band.

The Bridgeville Band poses for a group photograph in 1892.

Paris Lake on Hays Road was a popular vacation spot in the 1930s and 1940s. The getaway was located at the present site of Rossmoor Drive. This 1930s photograph depicts the rental cottages.

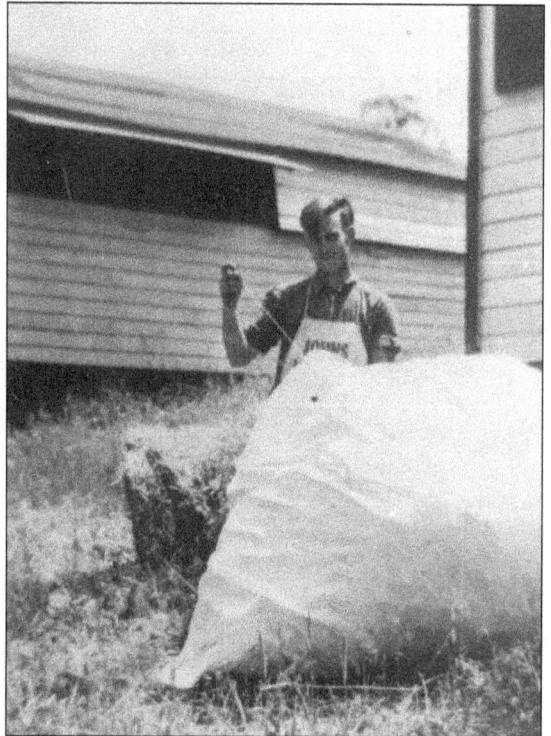

A man sews up a mattress filled with straw. These mattresses were used in all the Paris Lake cottages.

Children enjoy the Paris Lake pond in this 1946 photograph. The bathhouse is seen in the background.

OPEN
WEDNESDAYS
FRIDAY EVENINGS
SUNDAYS HOLIDAYS

Ann (left) and Leigh Gerstenberger enjoy the Pony Ring in the 1950s. The Pony Ring was located at the entrance to Rolling Meadows North.

Guests gather for a noon dinner party at the home of Mr. and Mrs. John Gilfillan on Washington Road c. 1900. Mrs. Gilfillan is in the front row on the far left.

Folks enjoy a game of croquet at the John T. Fife home c. 1900. John T. Fife is seated under the tree.

Mrs. Alexander Gilfillan hosted a fancywork party at her home on Swanson Lane. Mrs. Gilfillan is holding a baby (third row, far left).

The Gilfillan family held a reunion in 1884 at the Alexander Gilfillan home on Swanson Lane. An easy chair was presented to 85-year-old Aunt Betsy Wallace (front row, center).

The descendants of Christian Lesnett assembled for a family reunion in August 1908.

The McEwen home, on Locust Lane, was the scene of a 1920 reunion of the Smith and McEwen families.

The annual Poellot family reunion was held at the home of George and Ida May Poellot on Boyce Road. Local families represented here are Poellot, Patton, Godwin, Wycoff, and Walther. This photograph was taken in July 1955.

The ladies of Bethel Presbyterian Church are pictured here as they go to a picnic in the 1920s.

Children are shown lined up near the Lutz home on Washington Avenue in Bridgeville for the 1898 Independence Day parade.

Three Fife sisters-in-law enjoy watermelon at a picnic. From left to right are Edna, wife of Sam; Ruth, wife of Bill; and Ruth, wife of John.

Ralph Godwin (left) and Chuck Buzzatto proudly display the fish they caught.

Dorothy Palombo Holden celebrates her second birthday with a birthday cake on the running board of the family car.

The Currie sisters proudly show their 1950 Packard on Upper St. Clair Community Day. They are, from left to right, Jane, Nellie, and Helen.

The Mooo Shop, located on the corner of Fort Couch and Washington Roads, was a popular gathering spot in the 1950s. It was famous for exceptional banana splits.

The new Gammons Restaurant was constructed in the 1960s at Clifton on the site of the John Poellot home. It had relocated from the corner of Washington and Fort Couch Roads. The Outback Steakhouse is the current occupant of this building.

The Hi-Ho Supper Club was a well-known nightspot from the 1940s to the 1960s. Previously known as the Casa Loma, it featured the popular trio Jimmy Foots and Spickets.

Fort Couch was constructed to protect the pioneers from hostile Native American raids. The Whiskey Rebellion began here on July 17, 1794, as farmers and militiamen gathered to march on Bower Hill, Gen. John Neville's home, in protest of the federal tax on whiskey makers. The Pioneer Inn, pictured here, incorporated the original fireplace and walls from the fort. It was razed in 1985.

Seven

MEMORIES

The last passenger train pulled out of the Mayview station in 1953.

On March 15, 1937, TWA flight 15A crashed near McMurray Road where the YMCA now stands. All 10 passengers and the crew of 3 died in the crash.

The Cow Hollow Bridge—on Mayview Road, near Morrow Road—collapsed in the 1930s. It was never rebuilt.

The "Yellow Trolley" leaves the Upper St. Clair station on its way to Washington.

This 1940s view of the Drake Loop shows an interurban trolley on the trestle above as it speeds by on the way to Washington.

The intersection of Fort Couch and Washington Roads is featured in this 1947 aerial photograph. Hansen's Restaurant, which later became Gammon's, is the large white building on the corner. The plan of homes to the left of Fort Couch Road on Long and Adams Drives is English Village. The Green Lantern can be seen on North Highland Road in the upper left side of this photograph.

Carnegie Museum archeologists and volunteers excavated the Godwin-Portman site on Boyce Road in the autumn of 1978. A Monongahela Indian village was found along with an important burial ground. Artifacts from this site are preserved in the Carnegie Museum, Section of Man. A fictional story—"The Death of Flying Squirrel," by Richard George and Christine Davis—was inspired by these findings. The story was published in *Carnegie Magazine* in March 1982.

The Hays farm and Hays Road are seen in this 1930s photograph.

This view of Washington Road at the Gilfillan farm looks toward the present location of South Hills Village. Note the two-lane road and lack of traffic in the 1930s.

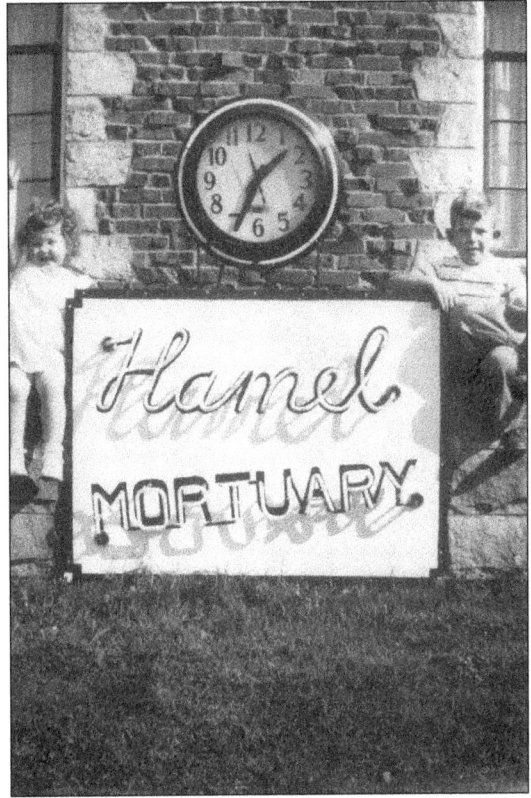

Dorothy and Milton Hamel Jr. pose by their sign and clock in this 1949 photograph.

Milton Hamel Sr. and Jr. survey their property on McMurray Road before the mortuary was constructed. The Drake trestle is seen in the background.

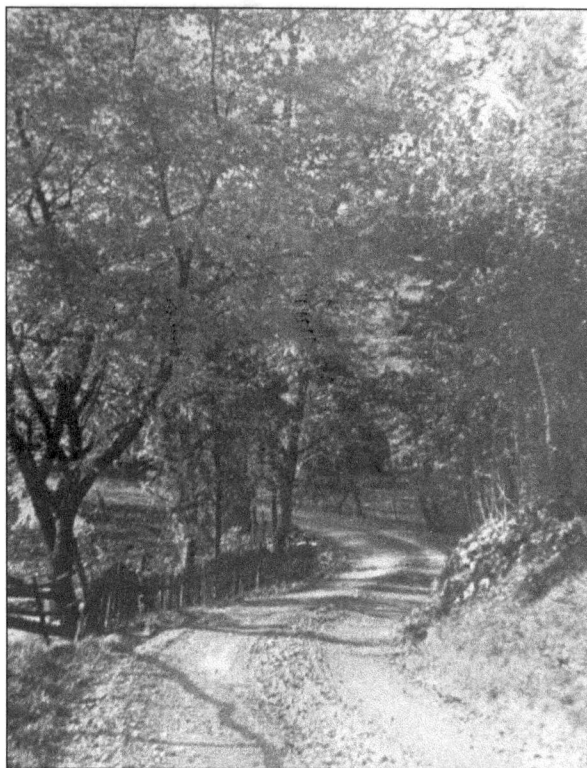

This is a view of Seeger Road near the Philips house.

This is Blind Lane, now called Hastings Mill Road, near St. Clair Country Club when it was an unpaved road.

www.ingramcontent.com/pod-product-compliance
Lightning Source LLC
Chambersburg PA
CBHW080910100426
42812CB00007B/2228